VISIONARY

ALAN HINES

Copyright © 2019 Alan Hines.

All rights reserved. No part of this book may be reproduced, stored, or transmitted by any means—whether auditory, graphic, mechanical, or electronic—without written permission of the author, except in the case of brief excerpts used in critical articles and reviews. Unauthorized reproduction of any part of this work is illegal and is punishable by law.

ISBN: 978-1-6847-0062-2 (sc)
ISBN: 978-1-6847-0103-2 (e)

Because of the dynamic nature of the Internet, any web addresses or links contained in this book may have changed since publication and may no longer be valid. The views expressed in this work are solely those of the author and do not necessarily reflect the views of the publisher, and the publisher hereby disclaims any responsibility for them.

Any people depicted in stock imagery provided by Getty Images are models, and such images are being used for illustrative purposes only. Certain stock imagery © Getty Images.

Lulu Publishing Services rev. date: 04/11/2019

Acknowledgements

Thank God for blessing me to live see another day, washing chaos away so I wont go astray. I cherish each moment, I bless the day.
As always I thank God for my grandmother, and my mother may they rest in Heavenly peace. Thank God for blessing me to release yet another book. I appreciate everyone that read one of my other books, I appreciate everyone that will read this one, God Bless.

Books of poetry already published by Alan Hines.

1. Reflections of Love
2. Thug Poetry Volume 1
3. The Words I Spoke
4. Joyce
5. Constant Visions
6. Red Ink of Blood
7. Beauty of Love
8. Reflections of Love Volume 2

Urban Novel already published by Alan Hines.

1. Book Writer
2. Queen of Queens

Upcoming books of poetry by Alan Hines.

1. Reflections of Love (Volume 2, and 3)
2. This is Love (Volume 1, 2, and 3)
3. Founded Love (Volume 1,2, and 3)
4. True Love (Volume 1,2, and 3)

5. Love (Endless Volumes)

6. Tormented Tears (Volume 1,2, and 3)

7. A Inner Soul That Cried (Volume 1,2, and 3)

8. Visionary (Endless Volumes)

9. In My Eyes To See (Volume 1,2, and 3)

10. A Seed That Grew (Volume 1,2, and, 3)

11. The Words I Spoke (Volume 2, and 3)

12. Scriptures (Volume 1,2, and 3)

13. Revelations (volume 1,2, and 3)

14. Destiny (Volume 1,2, and 3)

15. Trials and Tribulations (Volume 1,2, and 3)

16. IMMORTALITY (Volume 1,2, and 3)

17. My Low Spoken Words (Volume 1,2, and 3)

18. Beauty Within (Volume 1,2, and 3)

19. Red Ink of Blood (Volume 1,2, and 3)

20. Destiny of Light (Jean Hines) (Volume 1,2, and 3)

21. Deep Within (Volume 1, 2, and 3)

22. Literature (Volume 1, 2, and 3)

23. Silent Mind (Volume 1,2, and 3)

24. Amor (Volume 1,2, and 3)

25. Joyce (Volume 1,2, and 3)

26. Lovely Joyce (Volume 1,2, and 3)

27. Pink Lady (Volume 1,2, and 3)

28. Mockingbird Lady (Volume 1,2, and 3)

29. Godly tendicies (Volume 1,2, and 3)

30. Enchanting Arrays (Volume 1,2, and 3)

31. Harmony (Volume 1,2, and 3)

32. Realism (Volume 1,2, and 3)

33. Manifested Deep Thoughts (Volume 1,2, and 3)

34. Poectic Lines of Scrimage (Volume 1,2, and 3)

35. Garden of Love (Volume 1,2, and 3)

36. Reflection In The Mirror. (Volume 1,2, and 3)

Upcoming non-fiction books by Alan Hines.

1. Time Versus Life
2. Timeless Jewels
3. The Essence of Time
4. Memoirs of My Life
5. In my Eyes To See
6. A Prisoner's Black History

Upcoming Urban Novels by Alan Hines.

1. Black Kings
2. Playerlistic
3. The Police
4. Scandalous
5. The West Side Rapist

6. Shattered Dreams

7. She Wrote Murder

8. Black Fonz

9. A Slow Form of Suicide

10. No Motherfucking Love

11. War Stories

12. Storm

13. Ghetto Heros

14. Boss Pimps

15. Adolescents

16. In The Hearts of Men

17. Story Teller

18. Kidnapping

19. Mob Ties

1

Motivational Keys

The motivation I need to succeed,
to provide, feed.
Do good deeds.
Forever grateful of being freed.
Giving it my all at a full speed.
A given jewel, a planted seed.
Letting all the good and bad motivate me to succeed;
motivational keys

2

Efforts

Timeless efforts of not studying lessons,
brought forth stressing,
not realizing I should be counting blessings,
not stressing, but utilizing taught lessons.
No sins for confessions.
Bearing gifts, presents.
Accomplishing goals, by putting forth best efforts.
Being grateful for life, as living is precious.

3

Invisible, Visible

Invisible, but should've been visible, 3-d dimensional,
of intentions, hidden agenda of extended hand shakes
that's giving to you.
A secret meaning of text messages to you.

Couldn't see the invisible, obviously intentions,
suspiciously be-friend you.
Sometime the invisible becomes visible to,
other times invisible remains near sided to you.
You thought that they was a friend to you,
invisible to the scandals that women and men premeditate
and eventually do.

Invisible, and visible To

4

Differential

Clause,
Purpose,
Meaning,
Definition,
Defined as,
Surpassed,
Outlast,
Outcast,
Upper and lower class,
Happiness turned sad,
Good and bad,
Mom and dad,
Frowns and laughs,
Different laws passed,
Different generations as time passes.

5

Wisdom

Abolish all non sense giving.
Learn lessons from inmates in prison, that made bad decisions.
Be more understanding and listen;
accept constructive criticism.
Be grateful to be one of God's children, still living.
Enjoy wonderful feelings.
Stand tall as ceilings.
And control all dealings.
Properly raise children.
And let wisdom do all healing.

6

Life To Live

Too much life to live,
so I'm living better than it already is.
Head to the sky conquering fears.
I'm a grown man now so I whip away tears.
Not saying what I want, waiting on someone to give
going out to get it in the days of our lives,
throughout years.
I got my own life to live.
The man up above gave me this life to live so let me live.
But yet and still it is what it is in this life I live.

7

Tomorrow

Tomorrow will bring more better, brighter, beautiful things.
Living out our dreams.
Daily birds chirp and sing.
All hail to the new born king, and all the wonderful things another day tomorrow
brings.

8

I Must

I must continue breathing,
signing contractual agreements.
Twins and N'dia I must continue feeding.
Success seeking.
Leading.
Goodness breeding.
Allowing life to have it's meaning.

I must continue breathing, feeding,
knowledge seeking, to the word being obedient.
Proud to be one of God's creatures, and letting his
legacy live on through features.....

I must continue breathing.

9
Good Advice

At times you got to let go,
move on with life.
Realizing that you only live once not twice.
But always think twice.
Do what's right, make wise decisions come to life.
Do the good things you like.
Listen, follow, take heed to good advice.
When it's all said and done seek that place
formally known as paradise.

10

Remain

Remaining sane.
Keeping it simple and plain.
Living your own life doing your own things.
Chaos reframe.
Currency through success was gained.
Pleasant bells that rang.
The love, life, and loyalty was everything,
that remained.

11

God Is Great

God is good, God is great.
Thanks to him I was given life to live today, and yesterday.
Bombs, and semi automatic weapons they continue to create, but thanks to him I'm safe.
Rent is paid I have a pleasant place to stay.
For me a job and a publishing house he created.
Destine for greatness through his fate,
knowing that his everlasting love could never parish or wash away.
And I love and appreciate him more each day.
I definitley worship a God that for my sins allowed his only son's life to be taking away.
Oh yes I pray each day to an awesome God whom is good and great.....
God is good, God is great.

12

Heed

Sometimes but not all you must turn the other cheek.
In time the inheritance of the earth shall go to the meek.
You gotta swallow pride, take heed, lead to succeed.
Hard work brings forth achieve.
Knowledge is power that feed.
Be careful of the food you eat, the toxic air you breathe.
Let life be a lesson, learned, taking heed.

13

Fruitful

Be fruitful and multiply.
Wishing you'd live forever never die.
Keep your head to the sky;
as forever worship the creator above the sky.
Be grateful for the simple things that come by.
Just look at those in third worlds,
from hunger and lack of doctoring they die.
Love all, and trust none of any kind.
Keep working hard knowing some day you'll be fruitful,
and multiply, as a light shall shine.

14

Be

Let things be what they be.
Be observant, to see what you see, reality.
Allow inner spirits to be free from captivity.
Stand tall like the statue of liberty.
When it's said and done be who you be;
without trying to fit in to false proximity.
Be, be free.

15

Focus More

Focus more on spiritual guidance,
scriptual abiding.
Letting good intentions come out of hiding.
Top of the line presidential residing.
Displaying kindness.
Positive moves, smooth sailing, cruise control ridings.
Making wise decisions within deciding.

16

Subsidiary Rights

Non-fiction and fiction being brought to life.
Creatively write.
Red, blue, and black ink of sight.
Typing words all through the nights.
Peaceful uplifting stories, and others of violent fights.
Making it happen, not wondering what might.
Fans wondering when the next story will be orderable through sites.
Quaterly royalty checks being flown like kites.
Advancements of substantial likes.
Day and nights write.....
Controlling subsidiary rights.

17
Abstract

Abstract.
Snap back.
Statements of facts, is only an opinion not a fact.
Missing pieces of the map.
Those that left and wont come back.
Getting lives on track.
Trying to get the real thing back from being abstract.

18

Life Goes On

Stregthen my bones,
for those that's dead and gone.
I love and miss you, but life goes on, I must carry on.
Using the good qualities in you that was past along.
Often I see your kids and they're all grown.
Wish you was still here to live long.
Your legacy carries on.
But I must carry on.
Life goes on.

19

Replenished Beginning

Replenished beginning,
baptized, born again Christian.
Life without sinning, forgiving,
blessed to still be living.
With anew beginning, happy ending.....
Replenished beginning.

20

Momentarily

A momentary sign of relief.
Filing briefs, praying to the skies that appeals, and/or Habeous Corpus shall set 'em free.
Remembering those that's deceased, forever resting in peace.
Food for third world's to eat.
A place to be free.
A love of life to be.
Amazement never cease.
A momentary sign of relief.

21

God Gave

God gave me life,
courage, and sight.
Days I pray to him in the morning and nights.
God is my protector days within and even in the darkest night.
God gives me a vision, sight, a grip of light,
a path so I could be prosperous through his will,
and might.
God gave me life, courage, wisdom, understanding and sight.
He gave me life.....

22

As It Is In Heaven

Let it be done on Earth as it is in Heaven.
Give us this day as a daily bread.
Lets thank God in which we worship and thank him first instead.
Thank him for guiding us through to the straight path, and not leading us astray
as being misled.
Giving us the fulfillment of life to live breathing living, clothing, sheltered, sheild,
and fed.....
Let it be done on Earth as it is in Heaven, as food for thought,
as a daily nutrition of bread.

23

It Is

It is what it is.
God is the only one I shall fear.
Constant funerals of tears.
Living each day as a Merry Christmas, and a Happy New Year.
Knowing people and things, come and go, and disappear.
I live life as a realist sincere.
Each day I thank God I'm still living, still here

24

Letting Go

Sometimes you gotta let go.
It's no room, space, outta time to grow,
that poor performance considered as a relationship
you gotta let go, it's never going to amount,
never gonna grow.
People, places, and things you may love so,
but those that are no good, let go.
Give your ownself the love and respect to grow.

25

Be grateful

Be grateful to have a place to live.
To be a father or mother to kids.
Graduated to the new millennium;
another year still living here.

Be grateful, and sincere.

Be grateful that it is what it is,
still living still here.

26

Teach

Teach them how, in perfect harmony to sing.
To adore, love, appreciate the beautiful joy of life,
and what it could bring.
Ancient kings, and queens still in geans.

Teach, teach them how to sing.
How to keep the body, mind, and soul clean.
Pure as the nights for days exchange.

Teach, teach them how to study and learn, new, bigger, better and productive things.

Teach, teach them everything you know so they can achieve; teach the world to sing.

27

Positive

Always think positive,
delete, and unfriend the negative.
In your state of mind of living,
find you somewhere better to live.
Set good examples for especially the future of kids.
Be a product of what Heaven is.

Always think positive;
but remember to conquer fears, and face reality.
It is what it is.
Think positive and live.

28

Inspiration and Pride

Inspiration and pride,
wishing we could live forever,
didn't have to die.

Inspiration and pride.
It's good that some chose to get baptize,
be a product of Godly things behind close doors and above eyes.

Inspiration and pride allowed people to be good father and mothers to childs.

Inspiration and pride, live your livilyhood focused on staying alive.....

Inspiration and pride.

29

Enjoy

Enjoy, enjoying life at it's most highest of peak,
letting love for it be reached.
Be grateful to be able to live life free.
Tranquility and power of pursuit seek.

Enjoy, enjoy life be grateful for the life you keep, it is what it is.

Enjoy life in the days of our lives during years.

30

Fascinated

Fascinated by those that finish college,
and law school graduated; I congratulated.
Those that went for six and eight years finish,
finally made it.
At the end of the long awaited rainbow was a pot of gold
in history, for even today stated.
Performing on a positional positive related.

Briefly fascinated by the tight jeans,
and cute make up face prepareted;
but more interested, and fascinated with degrees you've created.
The future plans striving to make it.
With what class of lovers have you post dated.

Fascinated by each and every thing the Lord created.
Hoping I can meet and be with him after my fatal will be non negotiated.

31

Positive Lives

Positive, give positivity somewhere to live.
Turn the good dreams into reality, conquer fears.
Never stop the greatness, even through the blood sweat, and tears.
Keep, keep going on positively,
and always give the positive breath, to live.

32

Freed

Freed.
Freed from the places never wanted to go,
never wanted to see.
No more shall I be an alienated species,
now free as can be.
No third world poverty.
No more if, ands, and buts of probably.
No strange attachments of the falseness of friendships overlapping.
Freed minds from outragging, and senseless backtracking

33

One Way or The Other

In one way or the other we are all connected as sisters,
and brothers, intimate lovers,
work forces that are trying to go further.
Those that don't feel like being bothered.

Poets that create handwritten words that of an artist.
Godly creatures that were created in the likeness God, marvelous.

Through the creator one way or the other we are all sisters and brothers.

34

Pray

On the knees to pray.
Better days.
Happy holidays.
Problems washed away.
Cats and humans that wont go astray.
Bad memories fade.
Having faith in the Lord to have things his way.
Patiently awaiting judgement day.
But through it all must continue to pray.

35

God First

Put God first.
Let him be your doctor, healing nurse.
Let him cure sickness take away a curse.
Let him put money within bank accounts,
wallets, and purse.
God is the one that gives life through birth.
Let God have his way in Heaven, and on Earth.
Never go off your own understanding choose him first.

36

Guru of Legends

Guru of legends.
Learn from lessons.
Never accept a gift a free lunch as a present.
Mother and fathers raise kids, and enjoy each moment of their presence.
Live everyday of life as a gift of blessings.
Be your own guru of legends.

37

Equals

We should all be treated as equals.
Loving should be an on going sequel.
Always remeber we are all God's people.
Be fruitful, and free.
And be all you can be, equally.

38

It Is What It Is

Sometimes you gotta let things be what they is.
Stop shedding wasted tears.
Nothing we can do about mistakes from past years;
be grateful that you're still here.
Just learn from past experience rather they came from a far or near.
It is what it is.

39

Excuses

Excuses is useless it's nothing to it but to get up,
and do it.
Stop doing the same thing over and over again expecting different results,
that's fooloish; try something new.
Unto yourself forever remain and be true.
Get up and do the do, and stop making excuses.

40

Solomn Mind

Forever remain in a solomn mind.
Leaving all chaos, and madness behind.
Give sight to mental stages of being blind.
Love all and trust none of any kind.
Have peace within your heart and mind.
And success always seek for it strive,
and find.....
solomn mind.

41

Show

Show people how to lead, and teach.
Bring forth powerful messages,
be the word you preach.
Sing love songs, and let love melodies be reach.
Don't let the world affect who you be
live life with as much peace.
Show people the right path, lead, and teach.

42

Remembering

If you could remember a warming shelter in the coldness of Chicago's winter.
A pleasant view been seen from the neighbors windows.
Weddings of families and friends near you.
The ring boy presenting the ring,
as husbands and wives say, "I do."
Sneezes of God Bless You.
Love ones away from home we all miss and love you.
And those chasing dreams of success,
strive, and they shall eventually come true.
Remebering days of youth.
Remembering love that was gave and due.
Remembering the wonderful things in life we've been through.

43

My Own

I live on my own.
Build this pyramid of cement stone.
I live alone.
Far away from danger zones.
Creating stories that shall live on.
Trying to make money long.
Still remembering those that's dead and gone.
But I live alone,
living my life on my own in my own zone.

44

Mental Design

Design a place in time in your mind
where it's tranquil often at times.
Where dreams, and reality come together
as one to combine.
Spread love at it's best kind.
Create masterpieces of your own designs.
Let it be done down her on Earth as it is
in Heaven in the skies,
in your own mental designs.

45

Essence

Essence of time.
Make love to mines.
Attempt to be holy and divine.
Only changes is to get better with time.
Plants seeds of growth not only for yourself,
but for mankind.
Serve God knowing that Heaven is'nt hard to find,
everlasting life after your humanly flesh of a body decline.
Love your life the good, and the even the bad times.....
Essence of time.

46

Fullest

Fullest of life.
Those that's married be great husbands, and wives.
Treat others the way you want to be treated or even better, keep it polite.
Together as friends keep it tight.
Make even the slightest decisions be right.
Live you life down here as a version of paradise.

47

Next Level

Take it to the next level.
For less never settle.
Choas bury it six feet under the dirt with a shovel.
For goodness let it be no good byes, only hellos.
Let the brightness shine like purple, red, pink, and yellow.
Always atleast try, try to take it to the next level.

48

Positively Live

Think positive, giving negative no where to live.
Be a productive example on how you want your kids
to be groomed to grow to live.
Let love spread like the wings of an eagle that soared high in sky for hundreds of years.
Make dreams reality through dedication,
of hard work being sincere.
Always face reality, it is what it is.
Positively live.

49

Shed

Shed a sight, delight, less tears.
Know that God is the only one we should fear.
Let the days be merry like Christmas, and happy like new year.
Be blessed to still be living still here.....
Shed a light, and shed less tears.

50

We Shall

We shall be free, so let us be.
we shall spread love, thanks to the creator of all the
Earth, and Heavens up above.
We shall be a light, a light that must even shine in the night.
We shall be prosperous, prosperous is a must.

51

Insure

Insure to conquer, and explore,
endure, always wanted more.
Open up bigger, and better opportunities of doors.
An inner peace of your hearts core.
Unfaithfulness wanting no more.
Insure, conquer, explore.

52

Show Love

Don't judge or you shall be judged.
But love and you shall be loved.
Plant kisses, and hugs,
be a relief rescue for victims of hurricans,
and floods.
Balance out your equalibrium of finance to complete
those in need therefore, there of;
and do it genuinely, and don't worry your blessings will
come from the powers up above.

53

Good Deeds

Do good deeds.
Nourishment to feed.
Open up live some smell the fresh air, breathe.
Teach and lead.
No abortions breed.
Yes indeed, be a product of living life
prosperous, and free.....

54

Overcome

Overcome living in poverty of slumbs
transform into mansion on top of hills stun.
Be smart, don't make the same mistakes of being dumb.
Get out more, see the sights, live it up, have some fun.
Prepare for the future knowing greatness is to come.
Stepping over limitations, and boundaries to overcome.

55

Determined.

Wake up each morning determined.
Craving and yearning.
Study more do more learning.
Sit back and watch tables begin turning.
Give it your all, grand performing.
Never give up stay determined.

56

Remaining Forever True

In life people are not going to do the
same thing that you do for them to you.
Everybody hearts are different unto.
In life when you do good things just keep
doing what you do, remaining forever true.

57

Imperfections

Know that the creator made us all of our interior,
and exterior imperfect for the surfaces.
Knowing mistakes, and disbeliefs will occur.
Worhty and worthless.
Courages, other times scared and nervous.
The creator made us all imperfect.

58

Unto Thee

A sign of relief.
A less stressful way to be free.
The growth of a planted seed.
Noutrishing for mouths and minds to feed.
Better to give than receive.
Date those in which happiness can be acheived.
For each small or enormous blessing,
pray, and be pleased.
And let love be unto thee.

59

Life Line

A life line of happy people, happy times,
standing in bar-b-que, and amusement park lines,
party time.
Relationship in the night times,
men and women combine, entwine, each time.

A life line of support systems for those you love all the time.
Saying prayers for those trapped away,
those stuck in time.

A life line of happy feelings,
sweet dreams in the night time.
An everlasting light that shine.

60

Get Up

Get on up, and let your affections be all grown up.

Get on up and enjoy life to it's fullest,
doing things and having so much.

Get on up and go pass limitations of set goals and
boundary lines to succeed and to be
someone wonderful, and extremely just.

Get on up.

61

Thanks To Him

Thanks to him I shall never drown although I can't swim.
A light that shines when it's grim, my Father whom are in Heaven,
my truest friend.
Through him I awake to live again, and again,
having no fear of men.
Thanks to him my inner soul is beautiful within.
Everything I posses is thanks to him.

62

Beautiful Day

A beautiful day.
A beautiful way to get paid.
Being a part of the Lord's enchanting array;
never going astray.
Always having something good to say
as the sun shines your way.
Wishing everyday could be a beautiful day.

63

Proceeds

In need.
Indeed.
To breathe, offsprings to breed.
To manuevour, to proceed.
Chasing goals at top speed.
Not to much following lead.
Let nature take it's course as the creator
of the Heavens and the Earth proceeds.

64

The stars

Shoot for the stars.
Shine like the sun the crescent
fullness of the moon.
Blossom, peak throughout seasons, gloom.
Know that the Heavenly Father is coming
back to get the souls of his children soon.

65

Try Harder

Try harder, go hard.
Allow yourself to be your own candle light
that shines even in the dark.
Make the impossible become possible oxygen
upon Mars.
Be one of the shinning stars.

66

Liberated Free

The lands of liberty allow us to see.
Let us be free;
To roam the Earth endlessly.
Scholars, doctors, and professors let
us be.
Knowledge to it's highest degree.
Sights to see.
Power to achieve.
Power to receive.
Each one teach one lead.
To be powerful fathers to seeds.
To aim for the stars, and hands reach to please.
Liberated, free.
keep the faith and keep believing in our father God.

67

Get Up

Get up and grind.
Light your light,
of prosperity shine.
Chase after goals at all times.
Be that of holy and divine.

68

Never Change

Never change,
remain the same,
unless it's for better things.
Reign supreme.
Be the message you bring.
Joyously let your heart, mind, and soul sing.
Infatuate yourself with goodness you can bring.

69

Be Your Best

Be your best.
Lovely and bless.
Withstand the changing
of time as a passed test.

70

Be All

Be all you can be lovely and free.
Allow good times to repeat.
Stop thinking negative,
think positively.

71

Room To Grow

Create space and room to grow.
Through your heart and mind let love
be a continious flow.
Accomplish goals rather fast or slow.....
Room to grow.

72

Design Moments

Design precious moments within time.
Let your love shine.
Make peace be multipiled within hearts and minds.

73

Learning Experiences

Let mistakes be learning experiences.
Be a positive reflection
of what you see in the mirror.
To God be closer be nearer.

74

Give Sight To

Give sight to the blind.
Leave troublesome past behind.
Swim through infested waters
to show love to mankind.

75

Uplift Others

Uplift others.
Through God we're all
sisters and brothers.
Spread your wings of love,
and push others to go futher.

76

Finally

Finally it came a plus a gain.
Washed away counterfeit true colors of stains.
Praying under Jessu Christ name.
Prayers answered in due time of frames.
People finally utilized the powers
of the brain to enhance promoting
beyond range.

Finally it came wedding bells ring.
The birth of seeds as the church chorus sings.
Husband being treated as kings.
Wives being treated as queens.

Finally it came, me, I,
living out dreams.

77

Be a Visionary

Be a visionary.
Live life to the fullest,
be living but legendary.
Knowledge, wisdom, and
understanding to carry.
Give sight be a visionary.

78

Make Life

Make life be satisfying.
Gratifying.
Live life as the truth no denying.

79

Be Free To See

Be free.
Travel the Earth and
beyond, sights to see.
Be free to see what
the creator created for you
and me.

80

Make It Happen

Make it happen.
Be the ships captain.
Move forward no backtracking.
Love everlasting.

81

Live It, Earn It

Live it, earn it.
Chaos and madness set fire to
it burn it.
Live life and learn from it.

82

Days

Coming of days.
Loving in special ways.
Each day kneel down to God to pray.

83

Shine, Divine

Shine.
Be divine.
Help others get through troublesome times.

84

Cherish Life

Cherish life as a fulfillment of delight.
Accomplish goals as a nourishment of food for thoughts appetite.
Strive for excellence day, and night.

85

Believe

Believe.
Achieve.
Do good deeds.

86

In Time

In time be great.
In time be on time not late.
In time let God dictate
the pace.

87

The Love

Spread love.
On Earth, be Heavenly
like the Angels above.
Be that of Godly tendecies,
be that of love.

88

Shine and use

Shine and use your brain,
heart, and mind.

Shine let your light
gleam for a lifetime.

Shine be that of love
in between this and next lifetime.

89

Sweet and Simple

Sweet and simple.
My religious shrine, my holy
temple.
Loving that was plentiful.
Loving that was heart felt,
and beneficial.
She sweet and simple.

90

Celebration

Celebration.
Love that swept the nation.
Until death marriage permanently station.
No replacing.
Graduating.
Congratulations.
And threw the confetti up and
continue celebrating.

91

Stay The Same

Stay the same.
Never switch up
within lively time frames.
Be the one to orchestrate
things.
Let love and life
remain the same.

92

Be At Peace

Be at peace,
watch the sunrise
while facing the east.
Crush Satan dragon of the beast.
Stay on your knees to
pray daily to repeat.

93

Face The

Face the nation.
Let love be a permanent station.
Spread the wealth
of love that will be no replacing.

94

Love God

You must always love God.
Even when times are hard praise God.
The inventor of life beyond the stars.
Love, live, life worship God.

95

Near or Distance

Love from near or distance.
Presents felt through existence.
Be a reflection of artwork painting pictures.

96

Come Together

Come together united
as one we stand.
Never divided but united
grand.
Love again and again.
Come together as a purpose
to get goals accomplish
to make a stand.
Divided we fall united we stand.

97

Be A Shine In The Dark

Be smart.
Shine a light in the dark.
Allow God to be overwhelming
in your heart.
Be smart, sky rockets in flight,
a firely spark.

98

Enhance

Enhance.
Grow together live profound
rather woman or man.
Extend love freely genuinely
from hands.
Enhance shine like the son of man.

99

Be Rich

Be rich in your mind,
soul, and heart.

Be wealthy full of God.

Be rich in the way you treat
others from the start.

100

Visionary, Sight

Visionary, sight.
Lovely, delight.
The growth of seeds
to the air to take flight.

101

Wonderful Blessings

Bless to be living.
Wonderful feelings.
Love worth millions.

www.ingramcontent.com/pod-product-compliance
Lightning Source LLC
Chambersburg PA
CBHW071302040426
42444CB00009B/1832